The Story of the Sacred Harp
1844–1944

THE

Sacred Harp,

A COLLECTION OF

PSALM AND HYMN TUNES, ODES, AND ANTHEMS;

SELECTED FROM THE MOST EMINENT AUTHORS.

TOGETHER WITH

NEARLY ONE HUNDRED PIECES NEVER BEFORE PUBLISHED;

Suited to most Metres,

AND WELL ADAPTED TO CHURCHES OF EVERY DENOMINATION, SINGING SCHOOLS, AND PRIVATE SOCIETIES.

WITH PLAIN RULES FOR LEARNERS.

BY B. F. WHITE & E. J. KING.

PHILADELPHIA:
PUBLISHED BY T. K. & P. G. COLLINS,
FOR THE PROPRIETORS, B. F. WHITE & E. J. KING, HAMILTON, GA.
1847.

The Story

OF THE

Sacred Harp

1844–1944

A Book of Religious Folk Song
as an American Institution

by

GEORGE PULLEN JACKSON

VANDERBILT UNIVERSITY PRESS

NASHVILLE

1944

Copyright 1944
Vanderbilt University
Reprinted 2010

Frontispiece: Photograph of 1847 Imprint of First
Edition. Courtesy the Library of the Southern Baptist
Theological Seminary, Louisville, Kentucky.

Library of Congress Cataloging-in-Publication Data

Jackson, George Pullen, 1874-1953.
The story of the sacred harp, 1844-1944 : a book of
religious folk song as an American institution / by
George Pullen Jackson.
    p. cm.
ISBN 978-0-8265-1018-1 (cloth edition : alk. paper)
1. Sacred harp. 2. Hymns, English—Southern States—
History and criticism. 3. Church music—Southern
States. 4. Shape-note singing. I. Title.
ML3111.J3 2010
782.270975—dc22   2010025366

Contents

Old Baptist Music

Aside from the Holy Bible, the book found often-est in the homes of rural southern people is without doubt the big oblong volume of song called *The Sacred Harp*. It is not a church hymnal, though its contents are religious songs. Most of those who use it and know it well, if asked what sort of music it was, would answer: "Well, I reckon it's just Old Baptist song." Not a bad answer, this, despite the probability that the book was never used in Old or Primitive Baptist church services. But ask such people why it is called Old Baptist music, if the Baptists made it themselves or if they adopted it from elsewhere, and when, and where, and how, and why—and their answers, if any, would probably be vague and various.

This little book is intended to give answers to such questions. For the hoary *Sacred Harp* is now (1944) just a hundred years old, and it is therefore quite ap-propriate that those concerned with the remarkable volume should give some thought to its past.

The search for the beginnings of the types of song embodied in the *Sacred Harp* takes us back in time to a little before the birth of our United States, into the last years of the American colonies, or about 200 years ago. All Baptists were then Old Baptists. They were also country folk in the main and very much opposed to, and opposed by, those other religious denominations which centered in the few cities and towns along the eastern coast and were linked with the government. But the Baptists were growing fast in those days, perhaps *because* they were "the outs," the religious "leftists." And as they grew in numbers they grew also in their antagonism to all control either from the government or from any centralized religious (even Baptist) authority.

Freedom! Complete freedom of religion was the Baptist watchword. What wonder, then, that in the Revolutionary War for freedom from Britain, the Baptists played an extremely important part. What wonder, then, that after the war was won the Baptists who had suffered so grievously at the hands of the magistracy should be in the vanguard of those who saw to it that the new constitution of the new United States should guarantee them that freedom which they had so long striven for and so long been denied—the freedom to worship God according to the dictates of their conscience.

The new free nation was born. The Baptists found themselves not only free but inspired with unbounded zeal to develop their manner of worship independently, without any contamination from the older *established* religious orders.

One taint could come, they felt, from their singing the songs of the governmentally-linked denominations. The Baptists had not given much thought to group song in earlier times. Some congregations had not sung at all. So while Congregationalists, Presbyterians, Episcopalians, and Roman Catholics had sung psalms (perhaps *because* of this) the Baptists remained quite cold to psalm singing. But song was in the air. They had to sing something. So they decided, quite reasonably, to develop their own body of song. And this is just what they went about doing.

It was while George Washington was still alive that the country Baptists—then the fastest growing and soon to become one of the largest denominations—began to develop what we know now as Old Baptist music. The way they went about it was this: Their preachers collected a lot of hymns which had been written by Baptists or by those others like Isaac Watts, John Cennick, and John Newton whose religious ideas were much like those of the Baptists. These hymns they published without tunes in books like the *Dover Selection, Dossey's Choice, Mercer's Cluster, The Baptist Harmony* and Lloyd's *Hymns*. For many, many years these tuneless books were all they had and all they needed. Indeed, they didn't use even these as we do our hymnals now-a-days, with a book in every seat. Probably the preacher had a copy. But as for the rank and file, they depended on the preacher to "line out" the hymn and "hist" the tune, a practice which has not yet entirely died out among some groups, notably the negro Baptists. So from the point of view of the singers, the songs—and certainly their tunes—deserved the name "unwritten music"; and that is what they were called generally.

What was this unwritten music? What tunes did the preachers "tone" and everybody sing without ever having seen such melodies in notation? The *Sacred Harp* with its scores of Old Baptist tunes gives the answer. But it was not the first tune book of such music. The very first collection of that sort appeared forty years before the *Sacred Harp* was born; and, strange to say, it appeared among the backwoods Baptists of New England. It was Jeremiah Ingalls' *Christian Harmony*, published in Exeter, New Hampshire, in 1805. And still other books, before the *Sacred Harp* and after it, added to our store of that unwritten music, now written, with the result that we have today some 600 different recorded tunes of this type.

We have the tunes. But where did the Old Baptists get them? For nearly twenty years this question has bothered me. I can answer it now with a degree of certainty: By and large the Old Baptist tunes found in the old books of the *Sacred Harp* sort were and are melodies of England, Scotland, Ireland, and Wales. They are airs which have been sung for hundreds of years in those parts from which most of our forefathers came, and were brought by our forefathers to these shores—unwritten music, but fixed in the memory of those forebears.

But these remembered tunes did not have religious texts. They had been sung usually with worldly words—old love songs or ballets such as "Barbara Allen," "Lord Lovel," "The Bailiff's Daughter," "The Wife of Usher's Well," "and "Captain Kidd." And many of the remembered tunes, fiddle or bagpipe melodies for example, had no words at all. To such known and loved tunes as these the Baptists began to sing their equally beloved religious poetry. This was the way Old Baptist music came into being.

It may make the process of "spiritualizing" the older worldly songs clearer if I give an example. Take "Wondrous Love" in the *Sacred Harp*. Its tune and its stanzaic structure were borrowed from the worldly song about the famous pirate, Captain Kidd. The link between the two songs may be seen clearly if one sings the "Wondrous Love" tune to the following words:

> My name was Robert Kidd, when I sailed, when I sailed,
> My name was Robert Kidd, when I sailed;
> My name was Robert Kidd, God's laws I did forbid,
> So wickedly I did when I sailed, when I sailed,
> So wickedly I did when I sailed.

The "Captain Kidd" tune was already a very old and widely sung melody when it was picked up nearly 250 years ago and associated with the tale of the wild pirate who was executed in England in 1701. There were several forms of the melody, all of which had nevertheless a clear family resemblance. The "Wondrous Love" tune is one. Three other forms are "Mercy's Free" (*Original Sacred Harp,* p. 337), "Saints Bound for Heaven" (*Original Sacred Harp,* Denson revision, p. 35), and "You Shall See" (Jackson, *Down-East Spirituals,* No. 272).

One by one the sources of the Old Baptist songs in the worldly folk airs have been found. The search for the sources has been made easier by three circumstances: (1) Those who have been interested in recording the worldly folk songs have been many; (2) they began their labors much earlier than I did mine; and (3) they have recorded, in the Old Country and this, a very large number of tunes which I have been able to compare with their close kindred, the religious folk melodies.

So the answer to the questions, what the Old Baptist tunes were and where they came from, is sure. They were not to any extent "composed" tunes, those made by individuals. They were folk tunes, made and made over by ages of singing by the race from which we all have sprung. These tunes with their comparatively recently associated spiritual texts ("Wondrous Love" is probably not more than 125 years old) were sung lustily and without need of book or musical notation.

While religious music of the sort we have been discussing was developed first largely by the Baptists, as we have explained, they couldn't hold it. It was too good, too infectious. By Andrew Jackson's time it had spread also to other denominations. William Caldwell made this clear in the preface to his *Union Harmony* of 110 years ago (Maryville, Tennessee, 1834). He declared there that "Many of the tunes which I have reduced to system and harmonized have been selected from the *unwritten music* (italics mine) in general use in The Methodist Church, others from the Baptist and many more from the Presbyterian taste." And when we examine Caldwell's tunes we find them to be largely the same as those in other country books of the time and in the *Sacred Harp* of ten years later.

As the Old Baptist music spread into other denominations, it spread also into the all-denominational camp meetings. And in that environment it underwent a change which gave the world a new variety of the same music, one which became known as the "chorus song" or the "revival spiritual song," a sort which may be recognized by the much repetition in the texts through refrains and choruses. This song type is represented in the *Sacred Harp* by "The Morning Trumpet," "I Have a Mother in the Promised Land," "I Belong to That Band," "Old Ship of Zion," "Old-Time Religion" and many others. In this form few of the chorus songs were really Old Baptist; and this simply because that denomination leaned originally toward predestination and thus did not adopt the revival method of growth widely.

The chief practical reason for the development of the repetitive revival spiritual song was simply the combination of a great desire to sing with an equally great scarcity of books to sing from. We all know how more people will sing and sing louder when they are not bothered with a lot of verses which they can't or won't learn. And it was due to just these conditions that "The Old-Time Religion" and hundreds of other textually easy songs sprang from the big revivals which had their beginning in southern Kentucky around 1800 as camp meetings and quickly spread with the revival movement over the land. From these facts it is easy to see also why the negroes were quick to adopt precisely this simple variety of the white man's songs and to make them their own to such an extent that they have been looked on widely, although erroneously, as of negro origin,—as "negro spirituals."

I must mention also another kind of music. This kind was neither Old Baptist nor camp-meeting music nor even folk music. I refer to the "fuguing tunes" and their close relatives, the "odes and anthems" which are found in profusion in the *Sacred Harp* as well as all country song books in America for a hundred years before the *Sacred Harp* appeared. Where did the fuguing tunes come from? And how did they happen to get into the books of Old Baptist music? To answer the first question properly we must go back rather far.

As far back as 200 years before the *Sacred Harp,* that is 300 years ago, groups of singers in Europe and the British Isles had their greatest fun in singing a number of tunes at once. They called it "polyphony." Another sort of song-fun, one growing out of polyphony, was to have one voice start a tune and other voices come in one at a time, beginning the same tune a bar or two apart. This was somewhat like the older "round," but as it became stylized the different voices soon came together in good harmonic fashion and ended that way. This song structure became known as the fuguing tune form (from the Latin word meaning appropriately to flee). It became widely popular in Britain and later also in the singing schools of the American colonies and remained so till some time after the Revolutionary War. William Billings' fuguing tunes, many of which are to be found in the *Sacred Harp,* are typical of the compositions of scores of New England musicians which filled the numerous singing school song books of the northeast.

Now for an answer to the second question: how did the fuguing tunes happen to get into the southern books of Old Baptist music? This is how it came about: The Old Baptists, as we have seen, had no *written-*musical tradition of their own. So when they went about the establishment of such a tradition, that is, of putting their own songs into notation, nothing was more natural than that they should adopt for its style of presentation the forms already established, the singing-school forms. So the Old Baptist music, never originally much more than a single tune affair, was dressed up in harmonic clothes—three and four parts. And once the Old Baptist singers found themselves and their songs in the singing-school atmosphere, nothing was more natural than that they should take over into their own collections also a selection of the most popular fuguing tunes, odes and anthems.

It was the backwoods Yankee, Jeremiah Ingalls, mentioned above as the first man to publish Old Baptist music, whose *Christian Harmony* contained the first mixture of that music with the singing-school fuguing songs.

It is somewhat hard to understand why this sort of song mixture, soon to be found in one book after another in the middle states and in the south, should have appeared first in New England where the Ingalls book was the first and the last of its kind. The phenomenon is best explained perhaps by the fact that while the movement of combining the two kinds of music was a general one in the American countryside, there were in the northeast strong influences coming from the cities which were antagonistic to *both* sorts and which tended to alienate even the country people from them, while in the other parts of the land, these home-grown varieties of music were received with open-armed friendliness.

How the *Sacred Harp* Came to Be and How It Grew

Benjamin Franklin had been dead but ten years when the wife of a young farmer, Robert White, living near Spartanburg, South Carolina, gave birth to the first of their fourteen children and named him after the great American statesman. Benjamin Franklin White's schooling, three short terms, was quite meager according to today's standards. It was, however, about the average for those times when many boys acquired on their own initiative much of that education which has since been given over to institutions.

An important part of his self-acquired education was in music; for music, in those times, was a matter of singing schools here and there and, other than this, self-instruction. In the singing schools of Ben White's youth they may have been using any one of half a dozen good books of the sort we have just described. He may have learned his first music from Ananias Davisson's *Kentucky Harmony* (1815), Freeman Lewis' *Beauties of Harmony* (Pittsburgh, 1813), Allen D. Carden's *Missouri Harmony* (1820); or he might have known even Ingalls' *Christian Harmony*

(1805) from copies which may have wandered southward.

But early in his musical career young White must have realized that he and his fellow Carolinians needed a book better than these, one which would contain also those many songs in their own southeastern "unwritten" tradition. Be that as it may, we find young White associated early with his brother-in-law, William Walker (they had married the Golightly sisters, Ben's wife being Thurza Golightly), in the compiling of just such a song collection. By the year 1835 it was finished and Walker took the manuscript to New Haven, Connecticut, where the book appeared that same year.

Just what happened at this juncture is not certain. But Joe S. James, in his *A Brief History of the Sacred Harp* (Douglasville, Georgia, 1904, p. 29f), tells that Walker, when he got to New Haven, seemed to forget completely that he had a brother-in-law and that the latter had done a goodly part of the work on the new book and that he deserved credit of some sort. But be the facts as they may, the book came out as "*The Southern Harmony and Musical Companion*, by William Walker" and with no mention at all of B. F. White. Mr. James was usually fairly correct in his statements. But he would himself doubtless have admitted that he presented but one side of the case.

This incident, according to James, caused White to pack up his worldly goods, leave friends and kin-

Benjamin Franklin White and Thurza (Golightly)
White. Photographed from a tintype of the
early 1870s in possession of the White family.

dred in the Spartanburg section, and move with his family to Hamilton, Harris County, Georgia. This was in the late 1830s.

In his new home White soon became a prominent citizen, editor of the official county newspaper, *The Organ*, clerk of the superior court of his county, and a leading teacher of singing schools there and in the country roundabout. And there it was that he commenced at once to make a new collection of songs. Many of these songs he published one at a time in *The Organ*; and the whole collection appeared in 1844 as *The Sacred Harp*, printed in Philadelphia "for the proprietors, B. F. White and Joel King." (See the frontispiece of this booklet.)

Higher up, on the title page of the *Sacred Harp*, the name "E. J. King" appears with White's name as joint author. Were E. J. King and Joel King the same man? James thought they were brothers, an opinion based on what he had been able to learn from the oldest *Sacred Harp* singers then living (1904). It is to be regretted that we are unable to tell more of White's associate in creating the notable book.

The *Sacred Harp* was widely used from the start. It was the official song book of the Southern Musical Convention (organized at Huntersville, Upton County, Georgia, 1845), The Chattahoochee Musical Convention (organized at Macedonia Church, Coweta County, Georgia, 1852), the Tallapoosa Singing Convention (organized in Haralson County,

Georgia, in 1867), and of countless other conventions organized during the following decades in the territory including Georgia and stretching westward with the tide of migration as far as Texas and Oklahoma.

Sacred Harp singing has never spread, as a real country institution, farther north than the southern reaches of Tennessee and Missouri. In the Carolinas the *Southern Harmony* and other books seem to have offered stiff competition. The most recently organized convention, one which is at the same time the farthest north, is the Tennessee Sacred Harp Singing Association, organized in 1939 and meeting in Nashville.

Major Benjamin Franklin White (he gained this title in the Georgia militia before the Civil War) died in Atlanta, Georgia, in 1879, and is buried in the Oakland Cemetery in that city beside his wife under a beautiful memorial stone set by kindred and *Sacred Harp* singers. James says that just before he died he sang plainly and distinctly "Behold, the morning sun begins his glorious way" (*Sacred Harp*, p. 391).

Among the offspring of B. F. White who carried on after their father ceased to labor were J. L. White, D. P. White, W. D. White, R. H. White, B. F. ("Frank") White, Jr., Mary Caroline (White) Adair, Nancy Ogburn (White) Byrd, and Mrs. E. H. Clarke. And these were followed in the work by large numbers of White's grandchildren and great-grandchildren, some of whom are still active singers today.

Among those prominently associated with the Whites were James R. Turner (b. 1807), J. P. Rees (b. 1828), H. S. Rees (his twin brother), I. M. Shell (b. 1826), Absalom Ogletree (b. 1819), Edmund Dumas, Leonard P. Breedlove, S. R. Pennick, R. F. M. Mann, E. L. King, E. T. Pounds, R. F. Ball, J. T. Edmonds, and Marion Patrick.

Among the leading singers of still later years, that is, toward the end of the nineteenth and in the early years of the twentieth century, James lists the following: Miles Edwards (b. 1822), J. M. Hamrick (b. 1838), Stephen James (b. 1821), Joe S. James (son of Stephen, author of the *Brief History* and chief editor of the 1911 edition of the *Sacred Harp*), C. H. Newton, J. A. Burdette, J. B. Henslee, Thomas McLendon, Mrs. A. J. McLendon, Mrs. W. C. Smith, W. S. Turner, J. H. Tyson, G. L. McEwen, Jesse M. Moseley, P. H. Chandler, J. E. Gurley, J. W. Dunford, T. B. Newton, S. P. Barnett, James Storey, J. M. Hutcheson, T. S. Andrews, J. M. Denson, and Tom Waller.

Members of the editorial committee which, under the guidance of the chairman, Joe S. James, revised and enlarged the *Sacred Harp* in 1911 were W. H. Bell, M. F. McWhorter, C. H. Newton, Absalom Ogletree, J. E. Eason, B. S. Aiken, J. C. Brown, M. D. Farris, J. G. Moore, J. H. Tyson, A. J. McLendon, T. M. Payne, J. W. Harding, G. B. Holder, S. W. Everett, C. J. Griggs, S. M. Denson, T. J. Denson, J. D. Laminack, G. B. Daniel, T. R. Newton, and J. W. Long. Together they present a cross section of leading singers, composers, and teachers in the *Sacred Harp* field around the turn of the present century.

The 1911 edition of the *Sacred Harp* was its fifth; the preceding ones having been made, after the first edition of 1844, in 1850, 1859, and 1869. With each edition the formerly published parts of the book remained practically unchanged. Merely a supplement of additional songs was added. Thus the original 263 pages of the book grew with the successive editions to 366, 429, 477, and 550. The chief change suffered by former editions at the hands of later editors was the removal of a score of older songs from the 1869 issue. Most of these songs, however, were returned to the book in the James edition of fifty years later and placed on their original pages, thus justifying the title of the later revision—*The Original Sacred Harp.*

Those just mentioned seem to have been all the important and straight-line editions during the 1844–1911 period. There was, however, another *Sacred Harp* which I cannot fully explain. It appeared in 1870, just one year after the edition which was sponsored by B. F. White, Dumas, Ogletree, Mann, and Patrick—a committee of "The Southern Musical Convention of the State of Georgia," in 1869. The preface to the 1870 book was signed by B. F. White alone and the book was copyrighted by him and D(avid) P(atillo) White, his son. Aside from the preface, the book is identical with that of the year before.

The 1870 book was reprinted in 1911 (same year as the James edition) and from the original plates but with a new supplement of 73 pages of song. The additional songs were different. They were *composed* music signed by such well known nineteenth-century musicians as William B. Bradbury, N. E. Everett, William Havergal, George Kingsley, Thomas Hastings, R. M. McIntosh, George F. Root, G. J. Webb, and Lowell Mason. The book is known as the "J. L. White edition" (after its chief editor) and is still in use in a number of Georgia and Alabama conventions. Sam C. Mann, a grandson of B. F. White, is active in its propagation.

Still another form of the *Sacred Harp*, widely used today in many states, more especially in the southern parts of Alabama and in Mississippi, Louisiana, Arkansas and Texas, is what is popularly known as "The Cooper edition." It was made in 1902 by W. M. Cooper of Dothan, Alabama, and was a frank attempt at the "correction" and modernization of the old book. It has appealed thus to those who feel that such changes are justified. The revision work was done by a committee the members of which were entirely different from those active a few years later in making the James and the J. L. White editions. The Cooper edition is now owned by Judge B. P. Poyner of Dothan, Alabama.

The latest authentic *Sacred Harp* is the "Denson Revision" of 1936. It was made by a committee consisting of Thomas J. Denson, Seaborn M. Denson, L. P. Odem, L. A. McGraw, H. N. McGraw, T. B. McGraw,

O. A. Parris, George H. Parris, George M. Maddox, Otis L. McCoy, Howard Denson, and Paine Denson. These were formed into the Sacred Harp Publishing Company, Inc., of which Howard Denson was president and Paine Denson, secretary. The financial load of this radical revision was lightened materially by the funds which Lonnie P. Odem generously devoted to the cause which he loved—still loves. Thomas and Seaborn Denson (of whom we shall have more to say presently) died while the revision was being made. The chief music-editorial work was shifted thus to the shoulders of Paine Denson.

The new *Sacred Harp* is based squarely on the James edition. But 176 rarely or never used songs of the latter book have been discarded, and 41 have been added. Some little violence was done also to the earlier page-placing of the songs. But the new song sequence has been accepted by singers with but a little initial confusion.

The Denson revisers have, however, not changed the *character* of the old book one whit. All the newly added pieces have that combination of traits which distinguishes *Sacred Harp* music from all other tonal types. According to my count, about three out of four of the newly added pieces are fuguing songs, composed largely by Densons and other living *Sacred Harp* musicians.

Six thousand copies of the Denson Revision have been printed in the last eight years; and most of them have already been sold. It is the book in general use, especially in the Georgia, Alabama, and southern Tennessee region.

If imitation is the sincerest flattery, the *Sacred Harp* folk should be pleased with *The Colored Sacred Harp*. For this book, edited by J. Jackson for the negro Dale County (Ala.) Musical Institute and the Alabama and Florida Union State Convention, and published in 1934 in Ozark, Alabama—is clearly inspired by the white man's *Sacred Harp* and its song tradition. It has the same oblong shape and dimensions, the same fa-sol-la solmization, four-shape notation and four-part harmonization, and the same sorts of song—Old Baptist, revival spirituals, and fuguing tunes. And despite the fact that each tune is signed by a "composer," I find many of them merely variants of the white *Sacred Harp* melodies. The white singers greet the singers of *The Colored Sacred Harp* and wish them success in their undertaking.

When the *Sacred Harp* was young it had to fight its way as one of a half-dozen song books of its sort or similar. William Walker's *Southern Harmony*, which I have mentioned, was its keenest competitor in Georgia and the Carolinas. And this book was followed by Walker's somewhat modernized *Christian Harmony* with its added grist of songs by Lowell Mason and others and with its 7-shape notes. In eastern Tennessee and northern Alabama competition was offered by the *Harp of Columbia,* a good 7-shape book by W. Harvey Swan and Markus Lafayette Swan which came out in Knoxville in 1849. Another excellent Georgia book, one which was however too bulky for wide use, was William Hauser's *Hesperian Harp* (1848). Large numbers of the lively revival songs or camp-meeting spirituals were published in two books: Walker's *Southern and Western Pocket Harmonist* (1845) and John Gordon McCurry's *Social Harp,* Andersonville, Georgia, 1855. It is also quite likely that many copies of the old, frequently reprinted *Missouri Harmony* were still in use in the *Sacred Harp* territory during the 1840s and 1850s.

These competing books have all but disappeared today. The *Southern Harmony* is the song book of one lone singing in Benton, western Kentucky. A few years ago the Benson singers, with the help of the federal Works Projects Administration, got out a 1,000-copy photographic reproduction of the 1854 edition of the *Southern Harmony.* On the fourth Sunday in May, 1944, they held their sixty-first annual *Southern Harmony* singing convention. The grist of new books may add years to the life span of their singings; but it shows no signs as yet of bringing new singing groups to life. The other William Walker book, *The Christian Harmony,* was obtainable up to a few years ago. There are a number of Alabama singing conventions still using it. Its Philadelphia publisher died recently; but a movement is on foot in Alabama, I understand, to have the old book reprinted from the original plates. The plates of Swan's *Harp of Columbia* are now held by The Methodist Publishing House in Nashville; but there has not been enough demand for the book during the past twenty years to warrant a reprinting. So the "Old Harp" singers, largely in eastern Tennessee, must be running short of books. Thus the *Sacred Harp* stands practically alone today in its unique angle of the musical field as a vigorously living book and institution.

Some Hearers Don't Like It. Why?

I want to speak now of *Sacred Harp* music as it is found on the page and as it resounds from a thousand singing "classes" in as many courthouses, school auditoriums, and country churches over many southeastern states on most Sundays and many "Saturdays before" throughout the year and the years. And I shall speak of it first chiefly from the casual listener's point of view. Not that the listener's judgment of this music is important. It is not. This is not listener's music. It is *singer's* music. Listeners at singings are comparatively few. By and large they are those sturdy country people who have grown up with this music, know it thoroughly, love it, but for various reasons prefer to listen, and this by hours on end. I shall not discuss the music from *these* listeners' angle. It is the casual, first-time hearer of the music that I have in mind, and I shall try to portray his reaction. For while it is not important it is interesting.

It is quite usual to hear first-time hearers say, after listening to a few pieces: "It all sounds just *alike*," or "It is all *minor* music," or "I can't hear any *tune* to it."

I shall not discard such criticisms as simply untrue and the result of pure ignorance. There are elements of truth and untruth in them. And I shall try to point out these elements.

Sacred Harp music is four-part music. The four parts have been composed in such a manner that each voice part is equally "eventful" and thus interesting to the singer. This is quite different from present-day usage in choral music where all voices play a role subordinate to the soprano and thus are reduced often to long strings of notes, monotonous in themselves. When the other parts are brought up to an almost equal importance with the melody, as in the *Sacred Harp*, this part is bound to lose a deal of the prominence which the modern ear feels it should have.

Another condition in *Sacred Harp* singing submerges the tune even more deeply. I refer to the practice of each harmonic part (except the bass) being sung by both men and women. This mixture of male and female voices on the same part gives *Sacred Harp* singing one of its distinctive qualities and differentiates it still further from the usual practice according to which the sopranos and altos must be women and the tenors must be men. The casual hearer does not like this quality; does not realize what it is due to. So he casts the music aside with the disdainful remark that "it all sounds just alike," or that he "can't hear any tune to it."

The other criticism so often heard is as to the music's being "all minor." This criticism is just not true. Fully half the songs in the *Sacred Harp* are major (or in the "ionian" mode) and while the rest are in varying degree minor-*sounding* and while many of them are cast in the "natural" minor there are few "harmonic" minor tunes.

I cannot go into a full proof of the above statement here. I shall simply say, by way of suggesting its truth, that a tune, to be surely harmonic minor, must contain the seven tones of that scale, with lowered third and sixth and with the raised seventh in full cadences. The lowered third is often met with. But the sixth is almost always omitted from otherwise minor-sounding tunes (if not from the other harmonic parts). And the seventh is nearly always *sung as a lowered or natural tone*, even though it may not be printed as such.

There is still another type of minor-sounding scale or mode met with here and there in the *Sacred Harp*. It is that scale which has the lowered third and seventh and the *perfect sixth*. This is what was called in olden time the "dorian mode." In its lower tones it sounds minor (due to the lowered third) and in its upper reaches it sounds major (due to its perfect sixth). It has been blurred in some instances in the notation because it was confused, by those who first recorded those old unwritten dorian tunes, with what they took to be "minor." But the mode comes out clearly in such beautiful tunes as "Wondrous Love" where the printed *d*-flat is sung regularly as *d*-natural. Other songs where the perfect sixth of the dorian mode is sung though not printed are on pages 38, 74, 126, 142, 183, 211, 300, 302, 396, and 447. As far as I have been able to find, the only tune in the *Sacred Harp* which is not only sung in correct dorian but is printed that way, too, is "Jordan's Shore" whose sixth was corrected, in the 1911 James edition, from the earlier wrong *f*-natural to an *f*-sharp by George B. Daniel.

In speaking of leaving out or neglecting the sixth of the scale in natural-minor tunes, we are reminded of other gaps or omitted tones in these old folk tunes. The natural-minor tunes often omit the second as well as the sixth. And the major tunes often omit the fourth and the seventh. In such instances we have left, as actual tones employed in the tune, a five-tone scale in its different forms—forms which are very old in the music of Europe and America and are found in the music of primitive peoples the world over. Over half of the tunes in the *Sacred Harp* are gapped. They are, that is to say, either five-tone or six-tone melodies. One familiar example out of the hundreds is "Plenary" (p. 162) which all will recognize as the old Scotch folk tune "Auld Lang Syne."

We must remember that the tones of the gapped scales are the *basic* ones historically, and that the two left out are the less important ones in melody and that they have entered our music in comparatively recent times. We must bear in mind also the fact that the fewer-note tunes are appropriate to a fewer-chord harmonic treatment. With these facts in mind we can easily understand the effect of the *Sacred Harp* songs on the understanding and sympathetic listener. They impress such a hearer as strong, manly music. There is no effeminate ear-tickling in the *Sacred Harp* songs. And this manly strength, this austerity even, may be another reason why the *casual* hearer, with ears tuned to modern major musical niceties, mistakes it for music that is "all minor."

There are still other noteworthy features of the *Sacred Harp* which demand a word of comment. Among these are the form of the book, its pages of "rudiments," and its unique notation.

Its oblong shape (7x10 inches) is that of all singing-school manuals of its time and for a hundred years before its time. It was made necessary by the demands of the notation (one voice only on each staff) and by the demands of harmony according to which the four voices were placed one directly above the other.

The twenty pages or so of "Rudiments of Music" at the beginning of the book represent a feature brought to America from England over 200 years ago. These pages also bring to our minds the times long before individual instruction in music was available to the masses and when the "penmanship schools," the "literary schools" and the singing schools were peers. In the singing schools the one book answered the pupils' needs in helping them learn how to sing and in providing them with a collection of song.

To many, the most interesting feature of the *Sacred Harp* is its system of solmization and the shaped note-heads which go with it. The *fa sol la mi* notes are Old English. Shakespeare was familiar with them and has mentioned them in a number of his dramas. The system came with Englishmen to America in earliest colonial times and remained for nearly 200 years as the only system of sol-fa'ing in use in this country, that is, up to a little over 100 years ago when the continental European *do-re-mi* system was imported into our eastern cities and slowly supplanted the Old English custom. Today the *fa-sol-la* has completely died out in Britain; so our use of it in the south and in the *Sacred Harp* represents its sole survival anywhere in the world today.

The shaped note-heads, on the contrary, are an American innovation. Their invention dates from just one year before B. F. White was born. In that year, 1799, two singing-school teachers, William Little and William Smith of upstate New York, decided that a differently shaped head for each of the four notes would make the teaching and learning of singing easier. So they had types made and published a song book, *The Easy Instructor*, the very first one to use the four-shape notation.

The book became widely popular especially in the middle states. And while the patent notation was all but completely shunned in the northeast, it spread from one songbook to another in the southern and western regions and quickly became the only musical alphabet which the masses of rural Americans could read.

In those rural regions where the *do-re-mi* system came eventually into use, the shapes kept pace with the change by increasing to seven; this is the standard notation in southern rural song books today with the sole exception of the *Sacred Harp*. A clear idea of the popularity of the seven-shape notation now, 145 years after the shapes were first introduced, may be gained from the fact that the great Methodist Publishing House prints year after year more song books in shapes than in round notes.

In every *Sacred Harp* singing we hear echoes of old-time singing-school practice when each song is sung first once through with the notes—the words following. This fidelity to the old tradition is entirely commendable. There are but two sorts of song where the notes seem less in place in conventions: in the singing of long anthems, where the notes seem to tire the singers, to say nothing of the hearers, and in those few very fast pieces like "Union" (p. 116) where the notes, different in each part of course, become a pretty bad jangle of sound. Otherwise, the notes and the shapes are a valuable birthright without which the *Sacred Harp* would not be the *Sacred Harp*.

The casual listener is apt to sum up his opinion of *Sacred Harp* music by calling it simply "old-fogy." Now let's see just what this means. The word "fogy" once meant a steward or caretaker. An "old" fogy was thus a tried and trusted one who took care of such things as were worth preserving. We assert confidently that the *Sacred Harp* songs are those musical goods worth preserving, and that their singers are the tried and trusted caretakers, the "old fogies," of those "old-fogy" goods. "Old-fogy" songs have good company: the language we speak, the clothes we wear, the food we eat, the houses we live in, the laws we obey, the God we worship. The English tongue we speak has changed but little in the past thousand years. Chaucer, one hundred years before Columbus discovered America, talked about "grouching" and "wetting ones whistle." The clothes we wear are about the same (aside from fads which come and go and from the fact that we don't make as many of them ourselves) as they have been for many centuries. The food we eat still comes in the main from our old-fogy gardens and fields as it always has; though Mr. Swift and Mr. Armour do help out a little. The houses we live in have some improvements which add to our comfort, but a room, a window, a stair, a door, a chair and a bed—the essentials—are as old-fogy as the hills. As to the laws we obey—they are as old as the human race. For over two thousand years they have remained basically the same—Roman law, English common law on down to the enactments of our own states. One law builds on the other. The word "law" means something laid down, to stay. Something very "old-fogy." The oldest and most changeless of all our institutions is our old-time religion, based on a changeless God, a changeless Jesus Christ, and the moral law which Christian people strive to obey. Few would actually call Christianity "old-fogy."

As to old-fogyism in song generally one might remark that people used to really *sing* such music, still do so in *Sacred Harp* circles. As song has been modernized, however, it is sung less and less. It is listened to, at best. And this is probably largely because for some reason it doesn't appeal to the mass of those who would like to sing. Singing is one of man's most wholesome activities. It is far better, one would think, for mankind to sing old-fogy songs than to remain silent, listen to "better" song, and let his God-sent gift of singing lapse into disuse.

I see the viewpoint of the casual hearer of *Sacred Harp* singing. I understand the reasons for his snap judgments as outlined above. Some of the country people themselves are inclined to agree with him. My advice to all such is like that given by "Uncle Tom" Denson at the beginning of one of his singing schools:

"If some of you don't like this music," he told them plainly, "all I've got to say to you is you'd better get out. If you stay here it's going to get a-hold of you and you *can't* get away."

"Uncle Tom" gives strength to my conviction that *Sacred Harp* music must be sung and not heard.

Three Densons: Seaborn M. ("Uncle Seab"),
his son Whitt, and (right) Thomas J. ("Uncle Tom").
Photographed at the Mineral Wells, Texas,
convention of the Interstate Sacred Harp Singing
Association in the summer of 1930.

The Singers

The *Sacred Harp* has always rested in pious hands. While it has never been linked officially with any denomination, its singers have always been devoutly and fundamentally religious. All singings are opened and closed with prayer. The traditional dinner-on-the-grounds is always "graced" likewise. When one singer calls another one "brother" or "sister" and the older ones "uncle" or "aunt" it has a real and deep significance. It means that *Sacred Harp* singers feel themselves as belonging to one great family or clan. This feeling is without doubt deepened by the consciousness that they stand alone in their undertaking—keeping the old songs resounding in a world which has either gone over to lighter, more "entertaining," and frivolous types of song or has given up *all* community singing.

The members of this "clan" used to gather, fifty years ago and before, by neighborhoods. With railroads more available, it became possible for those of many neighborhoods to foregather in bigger, more centrally located and longer conventions (up to three days). Gasoline transport has more recently encouraged visits and return visits of singers living long distances apart. Until the present war restrictions came, it was no uncommon thing, for example, to see a group from Georgia and Alabama at a Texas singing and to see Texas singers returning the visit later. To-day this neighborliness is practiced especially among singers of Georgia, Alabama, and Tennessee.

Musical families, I mean groups of blood kins-folk, have also been towers of strength in keeping the *Sacred Harp* going. I have already spoken of some of them. I could not, within the covers of this little book, mention all such families even if I knew them all, which I don't. It may help readers understand the situation if I merely name those families represented by the Manns of Decatur, Georgia, and other descen-dants of B. F. White; the Drakes and Cagles of At-lanta, the Aikens and the Bishops of Carroll County, Georgia, the McWhorters of Birmingham, the McGraws in three states, the Kitchens family of Jas-per, Ala., the Odems and their large and active group of related singers in Lawrence County, Tennessee, the Lovvorns of Carrollton, Georgia, the Parris family in Winston County, Alabama, the Laminacks of Cull-man County, Alabama, and the Densons who now spread over northern Alabama and other parts of the south. There is hardly a *Sacred Harp* family, moreover, which has not married into one or more of the others.

I wish to single out the Denson family because of its uniform faithfulness, its unusually long-lasting devotion and its valuable contributions to the *Sacred Harp*—for special mention.

The first edition of the *Sacred Harp* contained the "Christmas Anthem" composed by James Denson of Walton County, Georgia. L. P. Denson, a Methodist minister, brother of James and, we presume, also a good singer, moved to Cleburne County, Alabama, around Civil War times and established that branch of the family which included two sons, Seaborn M. (b. 1854) and Thomas J. (b. 1863). It was just seventy years ago, when the *Sacred Harp* was only thirty years old and when its author, B. F. White, was still active,—that young Seaborn Denson taught his first singing school from that book. His much younger brother Thomas also began to teach as soon as he was old enough. This activity alone, carried along to the very end of their lives, might well have earned for the two brothers the title some observers have given them: "deans of the *Sacred Harp*."

But their life accomplishments were much wider. In addition to the hundreds of singing schools they conducted and the thousands of singers they educated in southern states from Georgia to Texas, they were ever active in composing music of the *Sacred Harp* types. We see signs of this latter activity first in the 1911 edition of the *Sacred Harp* of which Seaborn was musical editor. There we find one piece signed by both brothers, three pieces composed by Thomas, and ten by Seaborn. Thomas caught up with his big brother in the matter of published compositions twenty-five years later. In the 1936 Denson Revision eight more of his songs appeared. They were largely fuguing tunes. He named three of them for prominent *Sacred Harp* friends: "Coston" (the late W. T. Coston of Dallas, Texas), "Ackers" (the family of Tom Denson's second wife), and "Odem" (Lonnie P. Odem, *Sacred Harp* patriarch of St. Joseph, Tennessee). In the 1911 edition there is also one composition by Amanda Denson, Tom's first wife. And three hundred twenty-seven songs which had had three-part settings were made into four-part harmonizations by the addition of alto parts composed by Seaborn. These then were some of the accomplishments of the second generation of *Sacred Harp* Densons.

The third generation has been more numerous, equally gifted and just as devoted to the old songs and their propagation, Seaborn's eight children have all been enthusiastic singers and/or composers. They are Ida (Denson) McCoy, Iva (Denson) Blake, Seaborn I. ("Shell"), James T., S. Whitt, Robert E., Evan E., and William Philpot ("Phil"). Two of Whitt's compositions are in the 1911 edition. Among Tom's eight musical children, Paine (a Birmingham attorney), Howard (in business in Tuscaloosa, Alabama), and Ruth (Denson) Edwards (a teacher in the public schools of Cullman), have been the most outstanding in *Sacred Harp* work. In producing the 1936 revision, Paine was, as we have already stated, the general music editor; and seven of his compositions appear on its pages. Howard's contributions were two songs. Other third-generation Denson contributors to this volume were Maggie (Denson) Cagle, Ruth (Denson) Edwards and Annie (Denson) Aaron with one composition each. Three other daughters of Tom Denson, all active singers, are Vera (Denson) Nunn, Violet (Denson) Hinton and Tommie (Denson) Maulden.

(I think it would be proper to call attention here to other notable contributors of songs to this last *Sacred Harp*, people outside the Denson family. Among these were the three McGraw brothers, H. N. [two songs], L. A. [three], and T. B. [four], L. P. Odem, O. A. Parris, A. M. Cagle, O. H. Frederick, John M. Dye, J. B. Wall, Lee Wells, B. E. Cunningham, W. T. Mitchell, W. A. Yates, and Elmer Kitchens.)

The fourth generation of the musical Denson Dynasty is now maturing with a number of excellent singers and composers. Those already treading worthily in the steps of their forebears are three of Seaborn's grandchildren, Owel Denson, Dalila (Denson) Posey, and Otis L. McCoy.

The fifth generation is coming on fast, prolifically and promisingly.

The Turn of the Century

The current year, 1944, is the centennial of the *Sacred Harp*. Its significance is being recognized at every singing convention big and little. Singers are looking backward over the historic years, looking roundabout and trying to assess the present state of their beloved institution, looking forward and wondering about the *Sacred Harp*'s destiny during the second hundred years of its life.

In looking backward the singers are gladly paying a tribute of gratitude and honor to B. F. White and his disciples who brought the *Sacred Harp* into being, and to those later venerable men and women who fostered it after White ceased his earthly labors. The descendants of the founder are planning for this summer a big centennial celebration to be held on or near the spot in western Georgia where the *Sacred Harp* was first used in convention. The descendants and friends of the late Seaborn and Thomas Denson are to hold a singing festival lasting the entire week preceding and including the fourth Sunday in September at Double Springs, Winston County, Alabama. The high point in the week's festivities will be the unveil-

ing of a granite memorial on the courthouse square
in Double Springs bearing the following inscription:

To the Memory of the Brothers
SEABORN M. DENSON and THOMAS J. DENSON
(1854–1936)   (1863–1935)

who devoted their lives and gifts to composing
and teaching American religious folk music,
as embodied in the *Sacred Harp*, in most of the
southern states but notably in Alabama

THIS STONE IS PLACED

in the midst of their field of labor by the loving
hands of their families, pupils of their singing
schools, and legions of singers and friends in the
summer of the year 1944

THE ONE HUNDREDTH ANNIVERSARY
OF THE SACRED HARP,

while
"Uncle Seab" and "Uncle Tom" sing on—
"Way over in the promised land."

America Discovers Its Own Songs

The old stand-bys are dying off. This is the way of the world. But it bereaves the living and fills them with doubts as to the coming years. Will there be other tireless and excellent teachers like "Uncle Seab" and "Uncle Tom" Denson? Will southern family and neighborhood groups keep on singing as of yore? We don't know the answers.

But there is one fact which may comfort lovers of the old-time sings: *The songs themselves will not die.* For musical people over the entire United States are coming to know them as they were never known before, and are coming to a recognition of their beauty. This recognition and the rebirth of interest in the songs have followed the appearance, twelve years ago, of the present author's book, *White Spirituals in the Southern Uplands*, in which the *Sacred Harp* music and singing institution were portrayed.

The new interest in this music has been shown chiefly by leading American composers and choral leaders. Among the new apostles of the old lore are Henry Cowell, Carl Buchman, Ellie Siegmeister, E. J. Gatwood, Don Malin, Melville Smith, John Powell, John Jacob Niles, Harvey Gaul, Hazel Gertrude Kinscella, Annabel Morris Buchanan, Hilton Rufty, and Charles Bryan. All of these have made and published excellent arrangements of *Sacred Harp* melodies in form suitable to modern choral groups. And some of them, like Henry Cowell, have made settings patterned consciously "after the sparse harmonies of the early American folk hymn," patterned, that is to say, after such harmonies as we find in the *Sacred Harp*.

Randall Thompson, director of the Curtis Institute of Music in Philadelphia, has interwoven *Sacred Harp* melodic themes with the music of his cantata, "The Peaceable Kingdom." Van Denman Thompson has done the same in his "Evangel of the New World" as has also Lewis Henry Horton in his "The White Pilgrim." Melodic material from the same source has formed the background of symphonic works by John Powell, Charles Bryan and Roy Harris, and of an organ fantasia, "Garden Hymn," by Arthur Shepherd. And Virgil Thomson wove several *Sacred Harp* tunes into his screen score for "The River," a government-sponsored picture.

A goodly part of the renascence has centered around the fuguing tunes. Jeremiah Ingalls and his peers, pushed aside for over a hundred years by the Better Music Boys, by everybody, indeed, but the *Sacred Harp* folk,—are now coming into their own. Prominent among the revivers of fuguing tunes are Miss Kinscella, Mr. Buchman, Clarence Dickinson,

Mrs. Buchanan, and Joseph W. Clokey. Together they have published dozens of the old "fugues" only slightly altered from their eighteenth-century forms.

An indication of the widening popularity of old American song as found in the *Sacred Harp* may be seen in one piece, "The Poor Wayfaring Stranger." It has been variously arranged and published. One choral arrangement of the beautiful melody, made by the present author and the late E. J. Gatwood, has enjoyed a sale of over ten thousand copies. And for years a noted ballad singer who calls himself "the wayfaring stranger" has broadcast a weekly radio program from New York and has used this song as his theme.

When *Sacred Harp* singers learn of all this enthusiasm for their old-time songs, shown by practically all leading native American men and women of music and extending to all parts of the land, they will, I feel, have reason to be hopeful as to the future of their beloved art.

www.ingramcontent.com/pod-product-compliance
Lightning Source LLC
Chambersburg PA
CBHW030512100426
42813CB00001B/11

*9 7 8 0 8 2 6 5 1 0 1 8 1 *